Global Spiritual Warfare Authority

Shadow Prayer Warrior
Bible Study

Copyright © 978-1-884785-04-7
by Pat Holiday, PhD.
Agape Publishers, Inc.

Web Page http://www.miracleinternetchurch.com/
Web page: http://www.patholliday.com

IMPORTANT LINKS
Become A MIC Member
Become A Global Prayer Warrior
MIC Radio Show
MIC Radio Chat
Global Prayer Warriors Chat
Dr Pat's Books-Amazon
Giving at Miracle Internet Church
Send Dontations By Mail

Amazon.com: Pat Holliday: Books http://amzn.to/1333LVI

All rights reserved. No part of this material protected by this copyright notice may be reproduced or used in any form or by any means, electronic or mechanical without written permission from the copyright owner: e book printed in the United States of America.

Chapter One 4

Nation Will Fall into Darkness 4
    EVIL MAKES HIMSELF A PREY 4
        THE HEIR, THE ADOPTION SON OF GOD 4

Chapter Two 8

God's Presence 8
    THE ARK OF THE COVENANT 8
        RULING POWERS OF JERICHICO 8

Chapter Three 11

The Son of God 11
    POWER OF THE HIGHEST 11
        ADAM WAS THE SON OF GOD 11
        TRANSFERENCE OF HIS IN POWER 12

Chapter Four 16

Spiritual Warfare is Biblical 16
    OBEDIENCE TO THE GOSPEL SEEKING ENDUEMENT OF POWER 16
        BELIEVERS IN CHRIST ONLY 17

Chapter Five 21

He is our Battle-axe 21
    UNLIMITED POWER OF GOD 21
        OMNIPOTENCE, OMNIPRESENCE, OMNINISIENCE 21

Chapter Six 25

Luke Warm Churches 25
    HOT OR COLD 25
        SOME BECOME SHIPWRECK 25

Chapter Seven 29

Masters of Strong Delusions 29
    WITCHCRAFT – BLACK MAGIC 29
        Can Christians Be Hurt by Witchcraft or Black Magic? 46
        NATION FALLS INTO DARKNESS 29

Chapter Eight 31

Conquering Power 31
    SPIRITUAL DOMINION 31
        THE CHURCH OF JESUS CHRIST 31

Chapter Nine 33

Jesus Christ is a Living Sacrifice 33
    CHRIST INTERCESSION 33
        THE SPIRIT INTERCESSION 33

SCRIPTURES All KJV books 34

Strategies for Taking Territories 37

SCRIPTURES 37

ABOUT PAT HOLLIDAY, PhD 40

. BIBLIOGRAPHY 42

APPENDIX 1 45

Scripture on the Occult 45

FOOTNOTES 45

Chapter One

Nation Will Fall into Darkness

The Prophet Isaiah shows how the condition of the land when God does not have an intercessor. The entire nation will fall into darkness. However, God is faithful and He seeks for a man to accept the responsibility to stand before His throne to plead for His people. "For, behold, the darkness shall cover the earth, and gross darkness the people: but the LORD shall arise upon thee, and his glory shall be seen upon thee." (Isa. 60:2). Then we see in the previous chapter, Isaiah 59, "God pleading for someone to stand in the gap for His people."

EVIL MAKES HIMSELF A PREY

In Isa. 59:15-60, "Yea, truth faileth; and he that departeth from evil maketh himself a prey: and the LORD saw it, and it displeased him that there was no judgment. And he saw that there was no man, and wondered that there was no intercessor: therefore, his arm brought salvation unto him; and his righteousness, it sustained him. For he put on righteousness as a breastplate, and a helmet of salvation upon his head; and he put on the garments of vengeance for clothing, and was clad with zeal as a cloke. According to their deeds, accordingly he will repay, fury to his adversaries, recompence to his enemies; to the islands he will repay recompense. So, shall they fear the name of the LORD from the west, and his glory from the rising of the sun. When the enemy shall come in like a flood, the Spirit of the LORD shall lift up a standard against him. And the Redeemer shall come to Zion, and unto them that turn from transgression in Jacob, saith the LORD. As for me, this is my covenant with them, saith the LORD. My spirit that is upon thee, and my words which I have put in thy mouth, shall not depart out of thy mouth, nor out of the mouth of thy seed, nor out of the mouth of thy seed's seed, saith the LORD, from henceforth and forever.".

THE HEIR, THE ADOPTION SON OF GOD

When a sinner comes to Christ, he receives power to become a son of God. After salvation, we can receive all power from God.

"Now I say that the heir, as long as he is a child, different nothing from a servant, though he be lord of all; but is under tutors and governors until the time appointed of the father. Even so we, when we were children, were in bondage under the elements of the world: But when the fullness of the time was come, God sent forth his Son, made of a woman, made under the law, to redeem them that were under the law, that we might receive the adoption of sons. And because ye are sons, God hath sent forth the Spirit of his Son into your hearts, crying, Abba, Father. Wherefore thou art no more a servant but a son and if a son then an heir of God through Christ, how be it then, when ye knew not God, ye did service unto them which by nature are no gods. But now, after that ye have known God, or rather are known of God, how turn ye again to the weak and beggarly elements, whereunto ye desire again to be in bondage?" (Gal. 4:1-9).

ONE MEDIATOR

Jesus Christ is the only mediator between God and man, (I Tim. 2:5). His mission was fully accomplished. He is in full control and is exalted to the Father's right hand. He is the Master with almighty power. Jesus came to defy the power of Satan, (Acts 26:18). He challenged the rule of Satan, (Col. 2:10); conquered the right to dominion, (Col 2:14, 15). He set us free from the cause of sin, (I Pet. 3:18). He can set us free from the curse of sin, (I Pet. 5:10:11).

God's spiritual authority is the most astonishing power in the universe. The reign of Jesus Christ on earth with His saints is as sure as His birth, life, death, resurrection, ascension and High Priestly intercession. He has always wanted His disciples to participate with Him in spiritual warfare as is shown in the Scriptures.

THE LAMB OF GOD

Power from God After Salvation
Lord Jesus, You are the Lamb of God that takes away the sin of the world. You died for my sins according to the Scriptures. In You I have redemption through Your blood, the forgiveness of sin. Worthy

are You, the Lamb that was slain, to receive power and riches and wisdom and might and honor and glory and blessing . . . To Him Who sits on the throne, and to You, the Lamb, the blessing and honor and glory and dominion forever and ever." See (Jn. 1:29; I Cor. 15:3; Col. 1:14:14; Rev. 5:12, 13). 2

(Act 1:8 and 2:38) describes this extra endowment of power as the Baptism of the Holy Ghost.
People have the ability to influence others by the spiritual anointing that they walk under. (Acts 1:8), "But ye shall receive power, after that the Holy Ghost is come upon you: and ye shall be witnesses unto me both in Jerusalem, and in all Judaea, and in Samaria, and unto the uttermost part of the earth."

JOSHUA SAW JESUS

"Now when Joshua was near Jericho, he looked up and saw a man standing in front of him with a drawn sword in his hand. Joshua went up to him and asked, "Are you for us or for our enemies?" 14 "Neither," he replied, "but as commander of the army of the LORD I have now come." Then Joshua fell face down to the ground in reverence, and asked him, "What message does my Lord have for his servant?" 15 The commander of the LORD's army replied, "Take off your sandals, for the place where you are standing is holy. And Joshua did so." (Josh. 5:13).

MASTER'S PRESENCE

Joshua immediately recognized that he was in his Master's presence and he then submitted totally to Him. You see, being in His presence is an honor, a distinction that other religions don't get to have with their gods. Too often we Christians take Gods' presence for granted and we don't give it the reverence and honor that it deserves. The first thing that Joshua was told was "take off your sandals; you are standing on Holy ground." i

This is such a powerful illustration of Jesus working through a submitted person's obedience to His Word. Joshua saw into the spiritual realm a man with a drawn sword. He had to discern the supernatural spirit being and he knew that the war he was going to fight had to be fought by the power of the Spirit of God. He asked the Lord, "What message (Word) does my Lord have for his servant?" The secret to spiritual warfare knows the Lord's Word and believing His power will overcome all the power of the enemy and listening to His plan.

"Now Jericho was tightly shut up because of the Israelites; no one went out and no one came in. 2 Then the LORD said to Joshua, "See, I have delivered Jericho into your hands, along with its king and its fighting men. 3 March around the city once with all the armed men. Do this for six days. 4 Have seven priests carry trumpets of rams' horns in front of the ark. On the seventh day, march around the city seven times, with the priests blowing the trumpets. 5 When you hear them sound a long blast on the trumpets, have all the people give a loud shout; then the wall of the city will collapse and the people will go up, every man straight in." (Josh. 6:1).

Chapter Two

God's Presence

THE ARK OF THE COVENANT

After its creation by Moses, the Ark was carried by the Israelites during their 40 years of wandering in the desert. Whenever the Israelites camped, the Ark was placed in a special and sacred tent, called the Tabernacle. When the Israelites, led by Joshua toward the Promised Land, arrived at the banks of the River Jordan, the Ark was carried in the lead preceding the people and was the signal for their advance (Joshua 3:3, 6). During the crossing, the river grew dry as soon as the feet of the priests carrying the Ark touched its waters, and remained so until the priests—with the Ark—left the river after the people had passed over (Josh. 3:15-17; 4:10, 11, 18). As memorials, twelve stones were taken from the Jordan at the place where the priests had stood (Josh. 4:1-9).

RULING POWERS OF JERICHICO

The demonic ruling powers of Jericho had already bowed to the presence of Jesus before the walls fell because He had delivered the city for Joshua. However, Jesus always gives His servants the opportunity to be used as obedient spiritual vessels to share in the victory.

In vs 6 "So Joshua son of Nun called the priests and said to them, take up the ark of the covenant of the LORD and have seven priests carry trumpets in front of it. 7 And he ordered the people, Advance! March around the city, with the armed guard going ahead of the ark of the LORD. 8 When Joshua had spoken to the people, the seven priests carrying the seven trumpets before the LORD went onward, blowing their trumpets, and the ark of the LORD's covenant followed them. 9 The armed guard marched ahead of the priests who blew the trumpets, and the rear guard followed the ark. All this time the trumpets were sounding. 10 But Joshua had commanded the people, "Do not give a war cry, do not raise your voices, do not say a word until the day I tell you to shout. Then shout!" (Josh. 6: 6, 7).

BATTLE OF JERICHO

In the Battle of Jericho, the Ark was carried round the city once a day for seven days, preceded by the armed men and seven priests sounding seven trumpets of rams' horns (Josh. 6:4-15). On the seventh day, the seven priests sounding the seven trumpets of rams' horns before the Ark compassed the city seven times and, with a great shout, Jericho's wall fell down flat and the people took the city (Josh. 6:16-20). After the defeat at Ai, Joshua lamented before the Ark (Josh. 7:6-9). When Joshua read the Law to the people between Mount Gerizim and Mount Ebal, they stood on each side of the Ark. The Ark was again set up by Joshua at Shiloh, but when the Israelites fought against Benjamin at Gibeah, they had the Ark with them and consulted it after their defeat.

The Ark of the Covenant (Hebrew: אֲרוֹן הַבְּרִית ʾĀrôn Habbərît, modern pron. Aron haBrit), also known as the Ark of the Testimony, is a chest described in the Book of Exodus[1] as containing the Tablets of Stone on which the Ten Commandments were inscribed. According to the New Testament Letter to the Hebrews,[2] the Ark also contained Aaron's rod, a jar of manna, and the first Torah scroll as written by Moses; however, the first of the Books of Kings says that at the time of King Solomon, the Ark contained only the two Tablets of the Law.[3] According to the Book of Exodus, the Ark was built at the command of God, in accordance with the instructions given to Moses on Mount Sinai [4] In the Deuteronomy 5:6, these events are described as having transpired at Mount Horeb.[5] God was said to have communicated with Moses "from between the two cherubim" on the Ark's cover.[6] ii

PRESENCE OF GOD AND HIS WORD

Joshua and his army took the presence of God and His Word in obedience to the Lord to occupy and transform the city from powers of evil. Vs 20 Josh. 6: 21). "when the trumpets sounded, the people shouted, and at the sound of the trumpet, when the people gave a loud shout, the wall collapsed; so, every man charged straight in, and they took the city. 21 They devoted the city to the LORD and destroyed with the sword every living thing in it—men and women, young and old, cattle, sheep and donkeys."

PRESENCE OF MESSIAH JESUS

Jesus is Lord! He is the King of Kings and His word never fails. He is omnipotent!
We need to seek His presence. In order to do that, we need to be quiet and listen for Him to speak!

He is Holy. Revere Him, respect Him and recognize His authority! Recognize that you are standing on Holy ground

When He speaks, we need to not only listen, but you must do!

John 10:27-28 King James Version (KJV) 27 My sheep hear my voice, and I know them, and they follow me:28 And I give unto them eternal life; and they shall never perish, neither shall any man pluck them out of my hand.

James 1:22 "But be ye doers of the word, and not hearers only, deceiving your own selves."

We will NEVER achieve what God has for us if we refuse to listen to Him because it's "too much work" for us. God will NOT make every wall in your life come down easily though you will never know how many walls He already HAS blown down for you. Hear Him today; we are standing on Holy ground! iii

ABUNDANTLY THROUGH JESUS

"But after that the kindness and love of God our Savior toward man appeared, not by works of righteousness which we have done, but according to his mercy he saved us, by the washing of regeneration, and renewing of the Holy Ghost; Which he shed on us abundantly through Jesus Christ our Savior," (Tit. 3:4-6).

Chapter Three

The Son of God

POWER OF THE HIGHEST

"And the angel answered and said unto her, The Holy Ghost shall come upon thee, and the power of the Highest shall overshadow thee: therefore, also that holy thing which shall be born of thee, shall be called the Son of God," Luke 1:35.

"Luke 1:35 Context

"32He shall be great, and shall be called the Son of the Highest: and the Lord God shall give unto him the throne of his father David: 33And he shall reign over the house of Jacob forever; and of his kingdom there shall be no end. 34Then said Mary unto the angel, how shall this be, seeing I know not a man? 35And the angel answered and said unto her, the Holy Ghost shall come upon thee, and the power of the Highest shall overshadow thee: therefore, also that holy thing which shall be born of thee shall be called the Son of God. 36And, behold, thy cousin Elisabeth, she hath also conceived a son in her old age: and this is the sixth month with her, who was called barren. 37For with God nothing shall be impossible. 38And Mary said, Behold the handmaid of the Lord; be it unto me according to thy word. And the angel departed from her.

ADAM WAS THE SON OF GOD

There are several modes of being God's son. Lu. 3:38 says "Adam was the son of God". He was God's created son and received his life from God. 1 Jn. 3:2 says "Beloved, now are we the sons of God", (adopted sons through "Christ, who is our life" Col. 3:4). Jesus is the only begotten Son of God because no other human mother ever conceived by a work of the Holy Spirit, without a human father. Ben Weaver for verse 35

All descendants of Adam inherited the sin curse and passed it on to their children. As I see it, the only way God could have; adopted human children, is to by-pass the father role and to enter humanity to become a human mediator for us. Through the legal transaction of believing and confessing that God raised His Son Jesus from the dead for (me) anyone becomes God's son and heir along with Jesus (males and females alike).
Awesome grace!

SATAN COULD NOT KILL JESUS

The Holy Ghost shall overshadow three; Satan could not kill Jesus... when the time came, He gave up His Spirit! 1 John 3:16. Hereby perceive we the love of God, because he laid down his life for us: and we ought to lay down our lives for the brethren. From noon until three in the afternoon darkness came over all the land. About three in the afternoon Jesus cried out in a loud voice, "Eli, Eli, lema sabachthani?" (which means "My God, my God, why have you forsaken me?"). When some of those standing there heard this, they said, "He's calling Elijah." Immediately one of them ran and got a sponge. He filled it with wine vinegar, put it on a staff, and offered it to Jesus to drink. The rest said, "Now leave him alone. Let's see if Elijah comes to save him. And when Jesus had cried out again in a loud voice, he gave up his spirit. Sitting at the Right Hand of God."

RETURN TO CHRISTIAN VALUES

The Church of Jesus Christ must return to being the difference in every community. Jesus' Saints are His instruments on this earth because He is sitting at the right hand of God waiting and willing to give the power to win spiritual warfare. He gives a spiritual armor and weapons.
Our weapons are prayer, using His name, His blood, His Word and His power.

TRANSFERENCE OF HIS IN POWER

Paul shows this transference of His in power to usward who believe in (Eph. 1:19-22). And what is the exceeding greatness of his power to usward who believe, according to the working of his mighty power, which he wrought in Christ, when he raised him from the dead and set him at His own right hand in the heavenly places. Far above all principality and power and might, and dominion, and every that is named not only in this world, but also in that which is to come: And hath put all things under his feet, and gave him to be the head over all things to the church."

The problem is, some Saints never understand their position in Jesus Christ."

GRACE BY JESUS CHRIST

The Bible teaches grace as being of God, through God, all of God, the gift of God to an undeserving world, and God's grace is all sufficient

The believer is in Christ, and we are complete in him.

And ye are complete in him, which is the head of all principality and power," (Col 2:10).

"Therefore, all things are ours, for we are Christ and Christ are God's, (I Cor. 3:2-23).

"Blessed be the God and Father of our Lord Jesus Christ, who hath blessed us with all spiritual blessings in heavenly places in Christ. . ." (Eph. 1:3).

IT BECOMES OURS BY FAITH IN HIS REDEMPTION SACRIFICE

It becomes ours by faith in His redemption sacrifice.
> The law extended blessing to the good.
> But grace extends salvation to the bad.
> Here is set forth the totality of God's bestowment in Jesus.
> All Spiritual blessings are found in the Lord Jesus.

SUBMISSION TO JESUS

All spiritual blessing come to us through the Lord Jesus that leaves man out of it!

Jesus was the only man who ever completely pleased God, and the only way you and I can please God is through His Son.

"I am the way," (Jn. 14:6).

"I am the Door," (Jn. 19:9).

"Whosoever shall call upon the name of the Lord shall be saved," (Rom. 10:13).
"Neither is there salvation in any other; for there is none other name under heaven given among men, whereby we must be saved," (Acts 4:12).
"He is our salvation, our victory our sanctification, our redemption, and in Him we find rewards for our labors."

All of our righteousness is like filthy rags-therefore Christ the Righteous One becomes our righteousness, Inc. whom we have redemption Though His blood, the forgiveness of sins, according to the riches of His graces; wherein He hath abounded inwards us in all wisdom and prejudice," (Eph. 1:7, 8).

We are saved by "His marvelous grace," (Eph. 2:8).
We are led by His precious Sprit", (Rom. 8:14).
We are sealed by His Spirit until the day of redemption," (Eph. 4:30).
We are kept by His wonderful power, (Rom. 8:38, 39; I Pet. 1:5).
    We are saved because of God's love.

REGENERATION

The word "regeneration" appears only twice in the English Bible. Both appearances are in the New Testament. It was used once by our Lord in Matthew 19:28 and once by the Apostle Paul in Titus 3:5.

THE MEANING OF REGENERATION
The English word "regeneration" is the translation of palingenesia, from palin (again) and genesis (birth). It means simply a new birth, a new beginning, a new order. iv
When our Lord used the word, He said to His disciples, "Verily I say unto you, that ye which have followed me, in the regeneration when the Son of man shall sit in the throne of His glory, ye also shall sit upon twelve thrones, judging the twelve tribes of Israel" (Matthew 19:28). Here the Lord used the word in a wider sense when referring to His coming kingdom on earth. It is the time of the earth's

regeneration, the new order about which the prophets wrote, when Jehovah will set His King upon His holy hill of Zion (Psalm 2:6), "And He shall judge among the nations, and shall rebuke many people; and they shall beat their swords into plowshares, and their spears into pruning hooks; nation shall not lift up sword against nation, neither shall they learn war any more" (Isaiah 2:4; Micah 4:3). The coming kingdom of Christ on earth is the day of the earth's regeneration, (restoration of all things) Acts 3:21 (KJV) "21 Whom the heaven must receive until the times of restitution of all things, which God hath spoken by the mouth of all his holy prophets since the world began". (Acts 3:21). v

It is vital to believe the Gospel and the entirety it teaches for believers (II Tim. 3:16-17).
Faith in God's Word.

"All scripture is given by inspiration of God, and is profitable for doctrine, for reproof, for correction, for instruction in righteousness: That the man of God may be perfect, thoroughly furnished unto all good works," (II Tim. 3:16).

REPENTANCE AND RENUCIATION OF SIN

Repentance and renunciation of all sin and wrong doing is another requirement.
"To open their eyes, and to turn them from darkness to light, and from the power of Satan unto God, that they may receive forgiveness of sins, and inheritance among them which are sanctified by faith that is in me," (Acts 26:18).
"Wherefore come out from among them, and be ye separate, saith the Lord, and touch not the unclean thing; and I will receive you, and will be a Father unto you, and ye shall be my sons and daughters, saith the Lord Almighty," (II Cor. 6:17-18).

Chapter Four

Spiritual Warfare is Biblical

OBEDIENCE TO THE GOSPEL SEEKING ENDUEMENT OF POWER

"If ye then, being evil, know how to give good gifts unto your children: how much more shall your heavenly Father give the Holy Spirit to them that ask him?" (Lk. 11:13).

"And, behold, I send the promise of my Father upon you: but tarry ye in the city of Jerusalem, until ye be endued with power from on high," (Lk. 24:49).
See (Acts 1:4-15; 2: 38-39, 5:32).

Paul, a servant of Jesus Christ, called to be an apostle, separated unto the gospel of God." (Which he had promised afore by his prophets in the holy scriptures,) (Rom. 8:1-2).

"Making request, if by any means now at length I might have a prosperous journey by the will of God to come unto you," (Rom. 8: 10).

"Now I would not have you ignorant, brethren, that oftentimes I purposed to come unto you, (but was let hitherto,) that I might have some fruit among you also, even as among other Gentiles. I am debtor both to the Greeks, and to the Barbarians; both to the wise, and to the unwise. So, as much as in me is, I am ready to preach the gospel to you that are at Rome also," (Rom. 13-16).
See (Gal. 5:16-26).

"Let the word of Christ dwell in you richly in all wisdom; teaching and admonishing one another in psalms and hymns and spiritual songs, singing with grace in your hearts to the Lord." (Col. 3: 6:17). 56

BELIEVERS IN CHRIST ONLY
Spiritual warfare is a reality and is found in the Bible.

Acts 10:38 says, "How God anointed Jesus of Nazareth with the Holy Ghost and with power: who went about doing good, and healing all that were oppressed of the devil; for God was with him." Believers must learn to pray in faith.

"If any of you lack wisdom, let him ask of God, that giveth to all men liberally, and upbraideth not; and it shall be given him. But let him ask in faith, nothing wavering. For he that wavereth is like a wave of the sea driven with the wind and tossed. For let not that man think that he shall receive any thing of the Lord. A double minded man is unstable in all his ways," (Jam. 1:5-8).

"But without faith it is impossible to please him: for he that cometh to God must believe that he is, and that he is a rewarder of them that diligently seek him," (Hebr. 11:6).

ACCEPT GOD'S CALL
Believers must accept God's call as representatives of God.

But ye shall receive power, after that the Holy Ghost is come upon you: and ye shall be witnesses unto me both in Jerusalem, and in all Judaea, and in Samaria, and unto the uttermost part of the earth." (Acts 1:8).

GOD NEEDS YOU!
The world is in need of self-denying intercessors, people who will sacrifice their time for the church and the nation in prayer. Revival will come on the wings of prayer. We must return to God's way concerning the issues of our country. Territorial warfare must return to God's people to bring revival to the church. Moses' intercession is epitomized when he was chosen to lead God's people. He said, "O, this people have sinned a great sin, and have made them gods of gold. Yet now, if thou wilt forgive their sin, and if not, blot me, I pray thee, out of thy book which thou hast written."

Delivering Your Nation from Bondage

MOSES DELIVERED A NATION FROM BONDAGE

Moses delivered a nation from bondage of slavery and he was so devoted to his people, he was actually asking God to strike him dead and wipe his name out of the Book of Life! He was demonstrating that the number one reality of intercession is death to your flesh and love for the people. Many times, he is shown struggling in prayer because of the condition of his people.

GOD WILL FIGHT AGAINST YOUR ENEMIES

Deuteronomy 20:2-4King James Version (KJV)
2 And it shall be, when ye are come nigh unto the battle, that the priest shall approach and speak unto the people, 3 And shall say unto them, Hear, O Israel, ye approach this day unto battle against your enemies: let not your hearts faint, fear not, and do not tremble, neither be ye terrified because of them; 4 For the Lord your God is he that goeth with you, to fight for you against your enemies, to save you.

"So, will they fear the name of the Lord from the west and east. His glory from the rising of the sun; when the enemy comes in like a flood, the Spirit of the Lord will lift a standard against Him." (Isa. 59:1).

USE THE NAME OF JESUS

Name of Jesus accordance with Word of God And they must know their position in Christ. They have to learn to use the name of Jesus in accordance with the Word of God.

"And his name through faith in his name hath made this man strong, whom ye see and know: yea, the faith which is by him hath given him this perfect soundness in the presence of you all." (Acts 3:16:4:12---Acts 3:16).

Verily, verily, I say unto you, He that believeth on me, the works that I do shall he do also; and greater works than these shall he do;

because I go unto my Father. And whatsoever ye shall ask in my name, that will I do, that the Father may be glorified in the Son. If ye shall ask any thing in my name, I will do it. If ye love me, keep my commandments." (Jn.14:12-15).

"At that day ye shall ask in my name: and I say not unto you, that I will pray the Father for you: For the Father himself loveth you, because ye have loved me, and have believed that I came out from God," (Jn. 16:23-26).

JESUS AND THE BELIEVER
Jesus and the Believer
Paul shows the power relationship between the believer and Jesus' exalted position of authority. (Eph. 1:17-23). *"That the God of our Lord Jesus Christ, the Father of glory, may give unto you the spirit of wisdom and Revelation in the knowledge of him":* (Verse 17).

> Wisdom, Revelation and knowledge of Jesus.
> You must see Jesus from the Father's point of view.
> Jesus has already won the battle against Satan!
> He has authority to give you that same power!
> Seeing His exalted position gives you a picture of Satan's defeat!

"The eyes of your understanding being enlightened; that ye may know what is the hope of his calling, and what the riches of the glory of his inheritance in the saints," (Verse 19)
Knowing the hope of his calling is achieving the ability to overcome every dart of the enemy.
You can walk in your inheritance!

The Power of Jesus Christ
"And what is the exceeding greatness of his power to us-ward who believe, according to the working of his mighty power," (Verse 19).

> The Exceeding greatness of His power . . . His power is sovereign!

"And hath raised us up together, and made us sit together in

heavenly places in Christ Jesus," (Eph. 2:6).

His power is sovereign and He shares it with us!
Our position is from the vantage point of sitting with Him in Heavenly places.

Chapter Five

He is our Battle-axe

UNLIMITED POWER OF GOD
Sovereignty of God a theological term which refers to the unlimited power of God who has sovereign control over the affairs of nature and history, (Isa. 45:9-19; Rom. 8:18-39). The Bible declares that God is working out His sovereign plan of redemption for the world and that the conclusion is certain.

OMNIPOTENCE, OMNIPRESENCE, OMNINISIENCE
We are already sitting in heavenly place with our Lord.
"Which he wrought in Christ, when he raised him from the dead, and set him at his own right hand in the heavenly places," (Verse 20).

Immediately after the Fall, He talked about the curse of human sin and specified the cure for man's sin. To the serpent He said. *"I will put enmity between you and the woman, and between your seed and her seed; He shall bruise your head, and you shall bruise His heel,"* (Gen. 3:15).
The whole redemptive story of the Bible is the fulfillment of this prophecy by the sovereign God, as Paul clearly teaches in (Rom. 8-11).

The story of redemption from Genesis to Revelation is possible only because the sovereign God loves the created world, fallen though it is, and is able to do something about it. Without the sovereign love of the Father ministered to us through the Son and the Holy Spirit, there would be no really human freedom and no hope of everlasting life.2
God;

SITTING WITH HIM IN HEAVENLY PLACES

We sit with Him in heavenly places when we war against powers and principalities! (Eph. 2:6-7).

"And hath raised us up together, and made us sit together in heavenly places in Christ Jesus: that in the ages to come he might shew the exceeding riches of his grace in his kindness toward us through Christ Jesus." (Eph. 6,9).

We fight our spiritual warfare prayers from this advantage.
When you understand that Jesus delegates His power to you and then gives you the advantage of sitting with Him in heavenly places, you will win!

HE IS TRULY CAPTAIN OF OUR ARMY

"Far above all principality, and power, and might, and dominion, and every name that is named, not only in this world, but also in that which is to come: and hath put all things under his feet, and gave him to be the head over all things to the church, which is his body, the fulness of him that filleth all in all," (Eph. 21, 22, 23).

HIS NAME IS ABOVE ALL!
HIS POWER IS ABOVE ALL!
HIS LOVE IS ABOVE ALL!
KING OF KINGS

In the beginning, God spoke the word, and the universe came into existence!
At, and after the resurrection, Jesus displayed the power of appearing and disappearing and the power to rise unaided at His ascension.
Spiritual Warfare Confused with Demonic Bondage
Spiritual Warfare of the Flesh
Far too many people get spiritual warfare confused with demonic bondage. I believe this is because of the popular belief that Christians cannot have demons. Those in need of deliverance often think they are just in spiritual warfare, and its God's will for them to be harassed by the enemy. Nothing could be further from the truth!

THE ROCK AND BLOOD SACRIFICE

Jesus established His Church upon the rock of His blood sacrifice and the anointing and powers of the Holy Ghost. He believed that His Church should be able to wage a militant successful war against the powers of the Devil. His church was given the absolute ability to conquer the powers of darkness and win the souls that He had died for. He left His power for His people to be victorious because we have the same anointing through the Holy Ghost as Jesus did. Will you sleep during the greatest battle of the end tie Church while millions are in the valley of decision?

The Bible tells us, *"Ye shall know the truth and the truth shall make you free,"* (Jn. 8: 32).
The story of Ananias and Sapphira in (Acts 5:1-11), is a story of a possession or of a property that they sold and then gave the proceeds to the apostles. The problem was that they lied about the amount that was realized for its sale. They were in the flesh and not the spirit. The consequences of their lie were catastrophic. The apostle Peter said, "Whiles it remained, was it not thine own? and after it was sold, was it not in thine own power [*exousia* authority]?" (Verse 4).

WE HAVE AUTHORITY THAT WE RIGHTLY POSSESS

In other words, when we become Christians God doesn't want to take away everything from us. He has given us authority over the things that we rightfully possess. He wants relationship with us, He doesn't want to manipulate and dominate us. If He has us-our hearts, He has everything we possess. Actually, He doesn't need anything; He possesses all things.
What He really wants is us-a relationship with us. That is why we were born. However, the level of our relationship with the Lord will determine our lifestyles and our attitudes toward possessions.

AUTHORITY BEYOND OUR WILDEST DREAMS

What never ceases to amaze one is the fact that as Christians, God gives us authority beyond our wildest dreams. As His disciples, Jesus has delegated to us:

Authority to cast out demons "And Jesus gave

them power against unclean spirits to cast them out," (Matt. 10:1). Also, read (Mk. 3:15, 6:7,16: 17), and (Lk. 9:1). He gave you spiritual authority.

It is clear that each Christian possesses this authority.

Therefore, when you sense an attack of the devil on your body, your home, your relationships, and your finances or in any other area, you have the right to exercise your authority.

Chapter Six

Luke Warm Churches

HOT OR COLD
Either Hot or Cold
Jesus tells us that He detests Luke warmness in believers. If we understand the word cold to mean hostility to the Gospel, we must conclude that Jesus would rather see a person an antagonist than a half-hearted follower. Some scholars suggest that Jesus was thinking about two springs located near Laodacea C the hot mineral springs located at Hierpolis and the pure cold-water springs that were in Colosse. The hot springs were seen as possessing healing powers. The cold, invigorating springs provided refreshment. The Church at Laodicea brought neither healing to the spiritually ill nor refreshment to the weary. They were lukewarm and therefore no help to anyone. They were self-centered and living in the flesh. The problem with an average Christian is that he is just an average Christian. (Rev. 3:15).

The warfare of the saints is not after the flesh.
"For though we walk in the flesh, we do not war after the flesh: 4 (For the weapons of our warfare are not carnal, but mighty through God to the pulling down of strong holds.)" (II Cor. 10:3.4).

SOME BECOME SHIPWRECK
"This charge I commit unto thee, son Tim., according to the prophecies which went before on thee, that thou by them mightiest war a good warfare; 19 Holding faith, and a good conscience; which some having put away concerning faith have made shipwreck," (I Tim. 1:18 19).

STANDING AGAINST PRINCIPALITIES AND POWERS
The apostle Paul called it a good fight of faith.
"For we wrestle not against flesh and blood, but against

principalities, against powers, against the rulers of the darkness of this world, against spiritual wickedness in high places," (I Tim. 6:12).

IT'S AGAINST SATAN AND HIS DEMONS

"Lest Satan should get an advantage of us: for we are not ignorant of his devices," (II Cor. 2:11).

The Enemy Loves to Put Thoughts into the Believer's Mind. The enemy's thoughts (if meditated on), will generate strongholds which produces adversarial feelings. These powerful strongholds deliver you into a spiritual bondage which creates an incorrect discernment of who you are in Christ.

"I, even I, am he that blotteth out thy transgressions for mine own sake, and will not remember thy sins." (Isa. 43:25).

BABYLON PRINCE

The Prince of Persia, the territorial spirit of the first world order, Babylon, is raising his ugly head. This is the powerful principality that brought to a standstill Daniel's twenty-one-day prayer and fasting session from being answered. He was seeking God concerning the return of his people to their land after their long captivity in Babylon. God sent a mighty angel to fight against the Prince of Persia. This demonic power tried to stop the answer of Daniel's prayer from getting through by restraining God's angel in a spiritual warfare. This supernatural battle proves that even though the Principality over the country tried to stop his prayer, God sent His powerful angel Michael to battle this hindering fallen angel. These Scriptures reveal that Daniel had spiritual weapons. These weapons were repentance, faith in God, fasting, and prayers. This is the same Prince of Persia that is at war today in Iraq and he still rules the territory of the old city of Babylon.

NEW TOWER OF BABEL

You may remember it was in ancient Babylon that Nimrod and his Queen, Semiramis, built the Tower of Babel. Their goal was to unite all the people of the earth as one under the control of the pagan

Mystery Babylon Religion. Amazingly, the events of Babylon are now being repeated as humans honor its new" Tower of Babel", as the revived New World Order comes into view complete with one universal language and the trappings of a universal pagan religion.

Saddam Hussein saw himself as King Nebuchadnezzar II. He placed King Nebuchadnezzar I statues everywhere alongside his own. He even appears to resemble the first Nebuchadnezzar. Although Saddam has rebuilt the city of Babylon by restoring its gods, goddess and temples, he considers himself as the coming world leader, the Antichrist. However, he was rejected for that position by the powers of the world.

SUPERIOR MILITARY WEAPONRY

The Bush Administration went to war with Iraq and has superior military weaponry, but this was not a physical war. It was a spiritual war. Powerful spiritual beings are motivating it, their goal, to capture the city of Babylon for the city of the Antichrist. This was a war battling for territorial dominion to fulfill the book of Revelation, Chapter Eighteen. A great angelic spiritual war was unleashed and would take more than physical weapons to win it reminiscent to David in the Bible when he slew the giant affirmed, *"Thou comest to me with a sword, and with a spear, and with a shield: but I come to thee in the name of the LORD of hosts, the God of the armies of Israel, whom thou hast defied."*.

However, the attack on Babylon was stirred by the powers of Hell and greedy men and women who were seeking a new world order. God's people today must become spiritual, seeing events through the eyes of God to pray to defeat the armies of Satan.

The fact is this is a war that must be won! Satanic powers want America and the Christian Church of our Lord Jesus Christ to fail. The restoration of the city of Babylon was one of the "Signs of the Times", a warning to every true child of God of the approach-of the end of "the Age of the Gentiles". But regrettably because of the absence of warning from the Christian pulpits, thousands of God's children are entering these times unprepared to meet the barbarous attacks of Satan and his plan of releasing world-wide spirits of chaos.

Here's how you and I, working together can do our part to win the war on terrorism and best serve our nation and our God. The Church must be in intercession prayer during these dangerous days.

Chapter Seven

Masters of Strong Delusions

WITCHCRAFT – BLACK MAGIC
Come with me and I'll show you a winning strategy!
Can Christians Be Hurt by Witchcraft or Black Magic?
Dan Vander Lugt

Paranormal, World Religions:
Black
magic, magic, Neopagan, paganism, sorcery, Wicca, witchcraft

God is the Creator and Master of the natural world. Satan is only the master of illusion. He deals in hallucination and deceit. Any limited powers over nature he may possess are entirely circumscribed by God, but he can control susceptible minds. People in Satan's power are obsessed and hypnotized by evil. The source of black magic's power is fear. Academic writers have documented the life and death power of pagan magic over people who believe in it. vi

NATION FALLS INTO DARKNESS
Isaiah shows how the condition of the land when God does not have an intercessor. The entire nation will fall into darkness. However, God is faithful and He seeks for a man to accept the responsibility to stand before His throne to plead for His people. "For, behold, the darkness shall cover the earth, and gross darkness the people: but the LORD shall arise upon thee, and his glory shall be seen upon thee." (Isa. 60:2). Then we see in the previous chapter, Isaiah 59, "God pleading for someone to stand in the gap for His people."

NO JUDGMENT
In Isa. 59:15-60, *"Yea, truth faileth; and he that departeth from evil maketh himself a prey: and the LORD saw it, and it displeased him that there was no judgment. And he saw that there was no man, and*

wondered that there was no intercessor: therefore, his arm brought salvation unto him; and his righteousness, it sustained him. For he put on righteousness as a breastplate, and a helmet of salvation upon his head; and he put on the garments of vengeance for clothing, and was clad with zeal as a cloke. According to their deeds, accordingly he will repay, fury to his adversaries, recompence to his enemies; to the islands he will repay recompense. So, shall they fear the name of the LORD from the west, and his glory from the rising of the sun. When the enemy shall come in like a flood, the Spirit of the LORD shall lift up a standard against him. And the Redeemer shall come to Zion, and unto them that turn from transgression in Jacob, saith the LORD. As for me, this is my covenant with them, saith the LORD. My spirit that is upon thee, and my words which I have put in thy mouth, shall not depart out of thy mouth, nor out of the mouth of thy seed, nor out of the mouth of thy seed's seed, saith the LORD, from henceforth and forever.".

GOD NEEDS YOU

The world is in need of self-denying intercessors, people who will sacrifice their time for the church and the nation in prayer. Revival will come on the wings of prayer. We must return to God's way concerning the issues of our country. Territorial warfare must return to God's people to bring revival to the church. Moses' intercession is epitomized when he was chosen to lead God's people. He said, *"O, this people have sinned a great sin, and have made them gods of gold. Yet now, if thou wilt forgive their sin, and if not, blot me, I pray thee, out of thy book which thou hast written.".*

MOSES DELIVERS HIS PEOPLE

Moses delivered a nation from bondage of slavery and he was so devoted to his people, he was actually asking God to strike him dead and wipe his name out of the Book of Life! He was demonstrating that the number one reality of intercession is death to your flesh and love for the people. Many times, he is shown struggling in prayer because of the condition of his people.

Chapter Eight

Conquering Power

SPIRITUAL DOMINION

"All the cunning of the devil is exercised in trying to tear us away from the Word." Martin Luther.

God's spiritual dominion is the most astonishing power in the universe. God has always worked through humans to accomplish bring His kingdom to the earth. We must take heaven by force. Just as God gave the people of Israel the promise then told them to take it by force.

The Apostle Paul gave the Church the apocalyptic knowledge of the powers and principalities in Eph. 6. He disclosed that the church was in spiritual warfare and gave us the keys to spiritual warfare by using our spiritual weapons. Jesus Christ also told us in Matthew 11:12, *"The kingdom of heaven suffereth violence and the violent take it by force." Intercessors must break through the powers of darkness with spiritual military force warring against the kingdom of darkness.*

THE CHURCH OF JESUS CHRIST

The Church of Jesus Christ has to be the difference in every institution in the community. Jesus' Saints are His instruments on this earth as He is sitting at the right hand of God waiting and willing to give the power to win every spiritual battle. Remember our battle is never against flesh and blood and goal only concerns the spiritual condition of souls. We are not at war for gaining territorial lands or governments.

SPIRITUAL WEAPON AND SPIRITUAL WEAPONS

He gave the Church spiritual armor and weapons. Our weapons are prayer, using His name, His blood, His Word and His power. The

Apostle Paul shows this transference of Jesus' power to usward who believe in Ephesians 1:19-22, *"And what is the exceeding greatness of his power to usward who believe, according to the working of his mighty power, which he wrought in Christ, when he raised him from the dead and set him at His own right hand in the heavenly places. Far above all principality and power and might, and dominion, and every that is named not only in this world, but also in that which is to come: And hath put all things under his feet, and gave him to be the head over all things to the church."* The problem is some Saints never understand their position in Jesus Christ.

CHURCH REJECTED KNOWLEDGE

The Bible says, *"My people are destroyed for lack of knowledge: because thou hast rejected knowledge, I will also reject thee, that thou shalt be no priest to me: seeing thou hast forgotten the law of thy God, I will also forget thy children."* (Hos. 4-6).

Chapter Nine

Jesus Christ is a Living Sacrifice

CHRIST INTERCESSION

"Christ's priestly office consists of these two parts, (1) the" "offering up of himself as a sacrifice, and (2) making continual" intercession for us. "When on earth he made intercession for his people (Luke 23:34; John 17:20; Heb. 5:7); but now he exercises this function of his "priesthood in heaven, where he is said to appear in the presence" "of God for us (Heb. 9:12, 24)." "His advocacy with the Father for his people rests on the basis of his own all-perfect sacrifice. Thus, he pleads for and obtains the fulfilment of all the promises of the everlasting covenant "(1 John 2:1; John 17:24; Heb. 7:25). He can be "touched with the" "feeling of our infirmities," and is both a merciful and a" "faithful high priest (Heb. 2:17, 18; 4:15, 16). This" intercession is an essential part of his mediatorial work. "Through him we have "access" to the Father (John 14:6; Eph." "2:18; 3:12). "The communion of his people with the Father will" "ever be sustained through him as mediatorial Priest" (Ps. 110:4;" Rev. 7:17).

THE SPIRIT INTERCESSION

"(Rom. 8:26, 27; John 14:26). "Christ is a royal Priest (Zech." "6:13). From the same throne, as King, he dispenses his Spirit to" "all the objects of his care, while as Priest he intercedes for" "them. The Spirit acts for him, taking only of his things. They" "both act with one consent, Christ as principal, the Spirit as" "his agent. Christ intercedes for us, without us, as our advocate" "in heaven, according to the provisions of the everlasting" "covenant. The Holy Spirit works upon our minds and hearts," "enlightening and quickening, and thus determining our desires" "'according to the will of God,' as our advocate within us. The" "work of the one is complementary to that of the other, and" "together they form a complete whole.", Hodge's Outlines of" Theology.

See where <u>Intercession of the Spirit</u> occurs in the Bible...

"INTERCESSION OF SAINTS" in the KJV Bible

103 Instances   -   Page 1 of 4   -   Sort by Book Order

SCRIPTURES All KJV books

<u>Romans 8:27</u>
>And he that searcheth the hearts knoweth what is the mind of the Spirit, because he maketh intercession for
the saints according to the will of God.

<u>Daniel 7:22</u>
>Until the Ancient of days came, and judgment was given to the saints of the most High; and the time came that
the saints possessed the kingdom.

<u>Hebrews 7:25</u>
>Wherefore he is able also to save them to the uttermost that come unto God by him, seeing he ever liveth to
make intercession for them.

<u>Romans 8:34</u>
>Who is he that condemneth? It is Christ that died, yea rather, that is risen again, who is even at the right hand of God, who also maketh intercession for us.

<u>Jeremiah 7:16</u>
>Therefore, pray not thou for this people, neither lift up cry nor prayer for them, neither make intercession to me: for I will not hear thee.

<u>Jeremiah 36:25</u>
>Nevertheless, Elnathan and Delaiah and Gemariah had made intercession to the king that he would not burn the roll: but he would not hear them.

<u>Romans 11:2</u>
>God hath not cast away his people which he foreknew. Wot

ye not what the scripture saith of Elias? how he
maketh intercession to God against Israel, saying,

Romans 8:26
Likewise, the Spirit also helpeth our infirmities: for we know not what we should pray for as we ought: but the Spirit itself maketh intercession for us with groanings which cannot be uttered.

Isaiah 53:12
Therefore, will I divide him a portion with the great, and he shall divide the spoil with the strong; because he hath poured out his soul unto death: and he was numbered with the transgressors; and he bare the sin of many, and
made intercession for the transgressors.

Jeremiah 27:18
But if they be prophets, and if the word of the LORD be with them, let them now make intercession to the LORD of hosts, that the vessels which are left in the house of the LORD, and in the house of the king of Judah, and at Jerusalem, go not to Babylon.

2 Corinthians 13:13
All the saints salute you.

Romans 15:25
But now I go unto Jerusalem to minister unto the saints.

Psalms 16:3
But to the saints that are in the earth, and to the excellent, in whom is all my delight.

Romans 12:13
Distributing to the necessity of saints; given to hospitality

1 Corinthians 6:1
Dare any of you, having a matter against another, go to law before the unjust, and not before the saints?

Psalms 50:5
> Gather my saints together unto me; those that have made a covenant with me by sacrifice

Psalms 89:7
> God is greatly to be feared in the assembly of the saints, and to be had in reverence of all them that are about him.

Psalms 116:15
> Precious in the sight of the LORD is the death of his saints.

Psalms 132:9
> Let thy priests be clothed with righteousness; and let thy saints shout for joy.

Proverbs 2:8
> He keepeth the paths of judgment, and preserveth the way of his saints.

Daniel 7:21
> I beheld, and the same horn made war with the saints, and prevailed against them;

1 Corinthians 14:33
> For God is not the author of confusion, but of peace, as in all churches of the saints.

1 Corinthians 16:1
> Now concerning the collection for the saints, as I have given order to the churches of Galatia, even so do ye.

2 Corinthians 9:1
> For as touching the ministering to the saints, it is superfluous for me to write to you:

Ephesians 2:19
> Now therefore ye are no more strangers and foreigners, but fellow citizens with the saints, and of the household of God;

Philippians 4:22
> All the saints salute you, chiefly they that are of Caesar's household.

2 Thessalonians 1:10
> When he shall come to be glorified in his saints, and to be admired in all them that believe (because our testimony

among you was believed) in that day.

<u>Revelation 14:12</u>
Here is the patience of the saints: here are they that keep the commandments of God, and the faith of Jesus.

<u>Psalms 30:4</u>
Sing unto the LORD, O ye saints of his, and give thanks at the remembrance of his holiness.

<u>Psalms 132:16</u>
I will also clothe her priests with salvation: and her saints shall shout aloud for joy.

WINNING THE BATTLE FOR SOULS

It's time for Christians to look to Jesus and win the battle for souls.

Strategies for Taking Territories

Territorial taking power is shown in both the Old Testament and New Testament. It is not a new idea, only it is a strategy that has been lost too much of the Body of Christ. Territorial spirits take over for God can only be understood spiritually by a careful examination from the Word of God. Territories are shown as either under the power of God's people or under the power of Satan's servants. Territorial taking responds to the faith and obedience of God's servants. The subjection to Satan by his subjects slavishly holds territories and is moved by demonic supernatural powers or by supernatural beings.

SCRIPTURES

Bible Verses About Intercession of Saints
Bible verses related to *Intercession of Saints* from the King James Version (KJV) by Book Order

<u>Romans 8:34</u> - Who [is] he that condemneth? [It is] Christ that died, yea rather, that is risen again, who is even at the right hand of God, who also maketh intercession for us.

<u>Ephesians 6:18</u> - Praying always with all prayer and supplication in

the Spirit, and watching thereunto with all perseverance and supplication for all saints;

1 Timothy 2:1 - I exhort therefore, that, first of all, supplications, prayers, intercessions, [and] giving of thanks, be made for all men;

1 Timothy 2:5 - For [there is] one God, and one mediator between God and men, the man Christ Jesus;

Hebrews 7:25 - Wherefore he is able also to save them to the uttermost that come unto God by him, seeing he ever liveth to make intercession for them.

Hebrews 12:1 - Wherefore seeing we also are compassed about with so great a cloud of witnesses, let us lay aside every weight, and the sin which doth so easily beset [us], and let us run with patience the race that is set before us,

James 5:16 - Confess [your] faults one to another, and pray one for another, that ye may be healed. The effectual fervent prayer of a righteous man availeth much.

Revelation 5:8 - And when he had taken the book, the four beasts and four [and] twenty elders fell down before the Lamb, having every one of them harps, and golden vials full of odours, which are the prayers of saints.

Revelation 8:3-4 - And another angel came and stood at the altar, having a golden censer; and there was given unto him much incense, that he should offer [it] with the prayers of all saints upon the golden altar which was before the throne.

Revelation 8:3 - And another angel came and stood at the altar, having a golden censer; and there was given unto him much incense, that he should offer [it] with the prayers of all saints upon the golden altar which was before the throne.

Revelation 8:4 - And the smoke of the incense, [which came] with the prayers of the saints, ascended up before God out of the angel's hand.

ABOUT PAT HOLLIDAY, PhD

Patricia Holliday, PhD, was called into the ministry in 1975 and has ministered worldwide. She received her PhD at Southeastern Theology Seminary, Jacksonville, Florida, 1993. She is the President of Miracle Outreach Ministry. She appears on many international television and radio shows.

Miracle Outreach Ministries is an international ministry. Miracles, signs and wonders, healing, and deliverance follow this ministry. Her latest evangelistic trips include Ghana West Africa, Italy and Jamaica where many miracles happened.

Among her many political activities, she ran for the Florida State House of Representatives in 1972. She was elected State Committee Woman for her part and is a lobbyist in Tallahassee. She was a founding member and has officiated in many women's groups, Minute women of Florida, the Ponte Vedra Woman's Club, and the Four Foundation Inc., a home for non-delinquent girls in Duval County. She helped to organize two women's interdenominational fellowships. She has ministered worldwide in foreign lands. Dr. Holliday, is listed in Who's Who of the Woman of the World, Who's Who in America Politics, Dictionary of International Biography, Marquis Who's Who in the South and Southwest - Marquis Who's Who of American Women and Who's Who in American Religion Who's Who in America and Who's Who in the World.

Dr. Holliday is a member of the International Platform Committee as a noted lecturer. Recently she founded Miracle Outreach Ministries, a street church that feeds and clothes the poor. She is the author of the following books, Holliday for the King, Be Free, Born Anew, The Walking Dead, Signs Wonders & Reactions, The Solitary Satanist, Marriage Answers, New World Aftershock, New Age Humanism, and Entertaining Angels of Light, Can Women Preach?, Spiritual Warfare Armor, Spiritual Warfare Amour, Spiritual

Warfare Weapons, Battling Territorial Spirits, Transference of Spirits, Transference of Spirits, Devils Believe and Tremble, Experiencing Jesus, The Witch Doctor and the Man - Fourth Generation Witch Doctor Finds Christ!, Dancing On the Edge of Hell, Experiencing Jesus, Deliverance Manual Vol. 1 & 2, Family Deliverance Manual, Steps to Fasting, Spirit of Idolatry, Is Halloween Pagan?, New Creation, From Curses to Blessing Vol. 1, 2 & 3, Angel Fire, New Age Messiah, Baptism of the Holy Spirit, Women Messengers of Jesus Christ, Gods of the Stars, Healing is for Today, How to Be Born Again, Living on the Edge of Hell, Can Witches be saved? and Born Anew

. BIBLIOGRAPHY

Arnold, Clinton E Ephesians: Power and Magic (Cambridge, England, Cambridge University Press, 1989, p. 27.
Barnhouse, Donald Grey E the Invisible War, Zondervan Publication, Grand Rapid Mi., 180, Basham, Don, can a Christian Have a Demon? 1971: Whitaker Books. Deliver Us from Evil, 1972, Chosen Books. Bjornstad and Shildes Johnson, Stars, Signs, and Salvation in the Age of Aquarius, Bethany Fellowship, Inc. Minn.
Brooks, Pat, Occult Experimentation, (tract) 1972: Moody Press, Chicago. Catholic Encyclopedia.
Chafer, Lewis S. Systematic Theology, Vol 2, copyright 1947 by Dallas Seminary, Dallas TX.
Christensen, Larry, The Christian Family, 1970: Bethany Fellowship, Minn.
Expelling Demons by Derek Prince Publ. Ft. Lauderdale, Fl. 33302.
Charisma Magazine, Lake Helen, Orlando, Fl.
Clark's Commentary, Vol, 5, p 370, "LK.".
www.Demonbusters.com
Encyclopedia Britannica, art, "Easter".
The Eerdmans Bible Dictionary.
Ernest, Victor H., I Talked with Spirits, Tyndale House Publishers, Wheaton, Illinois.
Freeman, Dr. Hobart E., Angels of Light, 1969: Logos International Publishing Co., Plainfield, New Jersey.
Great People and the Bible, The Reader's Digest Association, Inc. 1974.
Gregory, Joel C., Gregory's Sermon Synopses, Broadman Press, Nashville, Tenn.
Frazer, The Golden Bough, p. 471. Frazer, The Golden Bough, p. 471.
Gasson, Raphael, The Challenging Counterfeit, Logos International, Plainfield, New Jersey.
Hislop, The Two Babylons, p. 103.
Holliday, Dr. Pat, Spiritual Warfare Manual # 2. The Walking Dead,

Be Free, Born Anew, Solitary Satanist, Witch Doctor and the Man-Fourth Generation Witchdoctor Finds Christ, Signs and Wonders and Reactions, Spirit of Idolatry Transference of Spirits, Miracle Outreach Ministry, San Jose Blvd., 2804, Jacksonville, Fl. 32257.

Jarman, Ray, Pseudo Christians, Logos International, Plainfield, New Jersey. Koch Dr. Kurt, Between Christ and Satan, 1962: Occult Bondage and Deliverance, Kregel Publications, Grand Rapids, Michigan.

Erica Joseph of Breakthrough Missions (address unknown) in a booklet titled "Sex with demons - Nightmares, Incubus and Succubus".

Layman's Bible Encyclopedia, Cleveland Tenn. Pg. 95.

Manuel, Francis D., Though a Host Should Encamp, 1971: Christian Literature Crusade, Fort Washington, Pennsylvania.

Martin, William G, Ma. A., B.D. The Layman's Bible Encyclopedia, The Southwestern Company, Nashville, Tennessee.

Martin, Walter, The Kingdom of the Cults, Bethany Fellowship, Inc., Minn. Minn.

The Gene and Earline Moody Deliverance Manual.

Irene Park, "The Witch That Switched", "Halloween & Pagan High Masses, Tampa, Fl.

Penn-Lewis, Jessie, and Roberts Evan, War on the Saints, Christian Literature Crusade, Fort Washington, Pennsylvania. Petersen, William L, Those Curious New Cults, Keats Publishing, New Canaan, Connecticut.

Roebert, p Stanley W. Fordsham, Smith Wiggleworth, Apostle of Faith, Sovereign World (Gospel Publishing House), pp. 109, 110.

Rex Shanks, CROWN OF LIFE MINISTRIES, Eyes of Understanding.

The Encyclopedia Americana, Vol 6, p. 623.

Philips, The Bible, The Supernatural and the Jews, World Publishing Company, New York, NY.

What's Your Question? On the Holy Spirit, Fasting, Healing, Glossolalia, and Demons, Ken Sumrall, Whitaker Books 607 Laurel Drive, Monroeville, Pennsylvania 15145.

Defeated Enemies, Corrie Ten Boom, Christian Literature Crusade, Fort Washington, Pennsylvania, 19034.

The Complete Guide to the Bible, Reader's Digest, Pleasantville, New York/Montreal.

Thomas, F. W., Kingdom of Darkness, Logos International, Plainfield, New Jersey.

Unger's (From the New Unger's Bible Dictionary. Originally published by Moody Press of Chicago, Illinois. Copyright (c) 1988.

Wilburn, Gary A., The Fortune Sellers, Regal, Glendale, CA.

Williams, Charles, Witchcraft, 1959, World Publishing Co. Cleveland.

Upham, Charles W., Salem Witchcraft, 1867: Wiggin and Lunt.

Whyte, Rev. H.A.M., The Power of the Blood, 1972, Dominion Over Demons, 1979, Pulling Down Strongholds, 1971, Hidden Spirits, 1970, Return to the Pattern, 1977, Fear Destroys, 1978, (booklets) Scarborough, Ontario, 2 Delbert Drive.

World Book Encyclopedia.

Wilkerson, Ralph, ESP or HSP? Melodyland Publishers, P.O. Box 6000, Anaheim, California, 92806.

Schwarze, C.T., The Program of Satan Good News Publishing Co. Weschester, 111.

Joseph Bayly What about Horoscopes? Arthur Lyons, The Second Coming, Satanism in America. Lindsey, Late Great Planet Earth, Satan is Alive and Well on Planet Earth.

APPENDIX 1
Scripture on the Occult

WITCHCRAFT: (Exod. 22:18, Deut. 18:18, I Sam. 15:23, II Kin. 9:22, II Chron. 33:6, Mic. 5:12, Nah. 3:4, Gal. 5:20).
ASTROLOGY: (Dan. 1:20, 2:2, 10:27, 5:57, 11, 15, Isa. 47:13, Deut. 4:19).
CHARMING: (Deut. 18:11, Psa. 58:5, Isa. 19:3, Jer. 8:17).
DIVINATION: (Num. 22:7, 23:23, Deut. 18:10, 14, Isa. 15:23, 28:8, II Kin. 17:17, Jer. 14:14, 27:9, 29:8, Ezek. 12:24, 13:6, 7, 19, 23, 21:21-23, 29).
ENCHANTMENTS: (Deut. 18:10, Exod. 7:11, 22, 8:7, Num. 23:23, 24:1, Lev. 19:26, II Kin. 17:17, 21:6, II Chron. 33:6, Eccl. 10:11, Isa. 47:9, 12, Jer. 27:9).
MAGICIANS: (Gen. 41:8, 24, Exod. 7:11, 22, 8:7, 19, 19:11, Dan. 1:20, 2:2, 10, 27, 4:7, 9, 5:11, Acts 19:19).
NECROMANCY: Deut. 18:11.
OBSERVING TIMES: (Lev. 19:26, Deut. 18:10, 14, II Kin. 21:6, II Chron. 33:6).
PROGNOSTICATORS: (Isa. 47:13).
SOOTHSAYING: (Dan. 2:27, 4:7, 5:7, 11, Isa. 2:6, Mic. 5:12, Josh. 13:22, Acts 16:16).
SORCERY: (Pharmakia) (Exod. 7:11, Isa. 47:9, 12, 57:3, Jer. 27:9, Dan. 2:2, Mal. 3:5, Acts 8:9, 11, 13:6,8, Rev. 9:21, 18:23, 21:8, 22:15).
WITCH or WIZARD: (Lev. 19:31, 20:6,27, Deut. 18:11, I Sam. 28:3, 9, II Kin. 21:6, 23:24, II Chron. 33:6, Isa. 8:19, 19:3).

FOOTNOTES

[i] http://www.sermoncentral.com/sermons/holy-ground-robert-cox-sermon-on-divinity-of-christ-105379.asp?Page=3
[ii] ibid
[iii] ibid

[iv] https://bible.org/article/regeneration-justification-and-sanctification
[v] ibid

[vi] Can Christians Be Hurt by Witchcraft or Black Magic?
Dan Vander Lugt

www.ingramcontent.com/pod-product-compliance
Lightning Source LLC
Chambersburg PA
CBHW032137090426
42743CB00007B/622